Antagonists in the Ch  Christian church. It is an _mini-
mizing destructive be envel-
ops a congregation.

THE REV. DR. RONALD WARREN
Memphis, Tennessee

Leaders of congregations should take this course because
it will make them *great* leaders, not just leaders.

BAIBA GUESS
Cordova, Tennessee

The material in the book is right on target. I believe this
course can do much toward restoring caring and effective
discipline.

THE REV. WILLIAM WITTIG
Lima, Ohio

I would highly recommend this course to every congregation. Being prepared for antagonists could preclude
many problems. I wish I had read the book 32 years ago.

THE REV. LEWIS GLICK
Muskegon, Michigan

Most congregations have neither understanding nor strat-
egy when destructive conflict erupts. This course will help
them "get some handles" on both—the result being a more
wholesome, healing, and positive ministry.

THE REV. JAMES WENZL
Wichita, Kansas

This study gave hope in a situation that seemed impossible. It also put tools in my toolbox, and insight!

MELANIE BUTTS
Peoria, Illinois

It is a great book. It will save congregations a lot of grief in the future.

THE REV. JOHN WEBER
Peachtree City, Georgia

I think every leader in all churches, no matter what denomination, should study this course so they will know what an antagonist is, and that there is a solution to dealing with them.

RUBY L. WARD
Muskegon, Michigan

I felt it was strong material with a Christ-centered flavor that the church needs.

THE REV. ROY HENDRICKSON
Albert Lea, Minnesota

The book is a must for every church worker to read. Districts and church bodies should encourage use of this study in every congregation.

THE REV. DR. DALE STURZENEGGER
Puyallup, Washington

It seems impossible to study this with just one group in the congregation. It is so important it should be taught several times with different groups. This is truly enlightening, extremely helpful, and in my opinion could be the saving of many congregations.

BLANCHE BIRD
Muskegon, Michigan

I plan on this being required study for elder orientation each year.

THE REV. JAMES CUMMINGS
Lakeland, Florida

Kenneth C. Haugk & R. Scott Perry

ANTAGONISTS
in the Church
STUDY GUIDE

Larry J. Russell

AUGSBURG Publishing House • Minneapolis

ANTAGONISTS IN THE CHURCH STUDY GUIDE

Copyright © 1988 Augsburg Publishing House

All rights reserved. Except for brief quotations in critical articles or reviews, no part of this book may be reproduced in any manner whatsoever without prior written permission from the publisher. Write to: Permissions, Augsburg Publishing House, 426 S. Fifth St., Box 1209, Minneapolis MN 55440.

Scripture quotations unless otherwise noted are from the Revised Standard Version of the Bible, copyright 1946, 1952, and 1971 by the Division of Christian Education of the National Council of Churches.

Library of Congress Cataloging-in-Publication Data

Haugk, Kenneth C., 1945–
 ANTAGONISTS IN THE CHURCH STUDY GUIDE.

 1. Haugk, Kenneth C., 1945–   Antagonists
in the church.   2. Church controversies.   I. Perry,
R. Scott, 1940–   . II. Title.
BV652.9.H373H38   1988   253   88-6390
ISBN 0-8066-2373-X

Manufactured in the U.S.A.   10-0373

  2   3   4   5   6   7   8   9   0   1   2   3   4   5   6   7   8   9

Contents

A Word from the Authors

*T*HIS study guide, for use with *Antagonists in the Church: How to Identify and Deal with Destructive Conflict* (Minneapolis: Augsburg, 1988), is our offering to congregations that want to achieve maximum benefit and learning from that book. The gravity of the subject matter makes "maximum learning" a worthy goal.

As authors, the two of us bring together the perspectives of a church professional and a lay person. Each of us has seen what a shambles unchecked antagonism can make of the mission and ministry of a congregation. We have written this guide out of that concern and out of our desire to help equip the servant people of God for individual and collective ministries.

This guide also reflects the insights and suggestions of those who read *Antagonists in the Church* and field-tested both the book and the study guide while both were still in manuscript form. A total of 24 pilot groups from 15 different denominations worked through the materials and provided us with extensive written feedback.

There is a very serious purpose behind *Antagonists in the Church,* and that serious purpose is reflected in this guide. But for all that seriousness, we do not think you will be bored by what you read. Whether you study this topic independently or as a group, we believe you will find it an extremely worthwhile learning experience.

We commend you for beginning. You join many other Christians who are working to strengthen and nourish Christ's kingdom of peace and healing. God bless your efforts!

KENNETH C. HAUGK   R. SCOTT PERRY

Introduction

ANTAGONISM is unhealthy for the church, and the word *unhealthy* doesn't begin to convey the depth of the problem. If you already have an inkling as to the truth of this, then you are ready for this course. If you haven't seen one or more antagonists in action, you can either take that statement on faith or test it later in this course. In any case, the prospect of dealing with the subject of antagonists and antagonism might be making you feel vaguely apprehensive. You might be hoping that a "nice guy" approach will work.

It won't. In a truly antagonistic situation, "You have met the responsible person, and that person is *you*" (to paraphrase Pogo).

When you have finished this course, you will know that dealing with antagonism is up to you. *Not you alone,* but you yoked with others in your congregation. Are you a participant in a study group or the leader of it? Are you a member of a congregation, a lay leader, or a church staff person? Whoever you are, it's up to *you* to prevent antagonism, to recognize it, and to deal with it when that becomes necessary.

By the end of this course, you will know *what* to do, *when* to do it, and, most especially, *why.*

You belong in this course. *It is all right to study this topic.* In fact, it is *essential* to study this subject to equip yourself for the sake of the continuing mission and ministry of the church.

Rationale

The fulfillment of the mission and ministry of the church necessitates that congregations *recognize* antagonism for what it is, *prevent* it where possible, and *confront*

7

it when necessary. Church staff and lay leaders have special responsibilities in this arena for working together, but the whole congregation has responsibilities as well.

Only Jesus Christ is strong enough to confront antagonists alone. As the church, Christ's body, his strength is ours, but only if we act as a body rather than individually. Too often, members of congregations have stood idly or helplessly by while a pastor or lay leader confronted an antagonist alone, usually to be badly hurt or destroyed, with serious consequences for the congregation as well.

Antagonism is real. And it can destroy individuals. It must not be ignored, but addressed purposefully and authoritatively by the whole church.

Purpose

One major task of the church is to equip the people of God for their work of ministry. Jesus' Great Commission reflected this when he commanded his followers to go forth and make disciples of all nations (Matthew 28:19-20). Making disciples is a many-faceted learning and growing process that starts with the people of God being equipped for the task (Ephesians 4:12). This study is intended to be part of that equipping process.

Ministry is either largely disrupted or greatly compromised when antagonism is occurring. It is therefore incumbent upon all responsible Christians to take measures to ensure that antagonism does not gain a foothold. The purpose of this course is to create in congregations caring Christians who are prepared to take all the necessary steps to put a halt to antagonism in the church, which in turn will allow congregations to get on with the business at hand—making disciples and caring for the needs of people.

This course will help you learn why encounters with antagonists are puzzling, difficult, and frightening. You will learn how to recognize antagonists early, how to prevent antagonism, and how to deal with it when that necessity arises.

Wider Applications for the Congregation

One of the participants in the pilot version of this course noted, "... the material here will be good for the church even if an antagonist never shows up!" Many suggestions are given for effective leadership and communications in general that will serve a congregation well in various circumstances. Particular chapters that are recommended for this purpose are Chapter 3, "Levels of Church Conflict"; Chapter 10, "How to Maintain an Anti-antagonist Environment"; Chapter 12, "How to Use Authority"; and Chapter 19, "Leadership Issues." Many other chapters contain helpful guidance for the general conduct of church business and individual interactions. They offer insights into how a congregation can be subtly turning people away and fostering inactivity.

Wider Applications in Everyday Life

Antagonism is by no means limited to church life! As individuals and groups dig into and work with this material, they are very likely to see applications for other areas of their lives—such as at work or within other organizations. Being able to recognize an antagonist can make all the difference in how you respond to an individual. Someone who is simply surly should get one response; an antagonist should receive another.

Once you have accurately identified someone as an antagonist, you can use what you learn from this study to respond effectively to that person. In fact, Kenneth Haugk has on numerous occasions conducted workshops on antagonism for people in business and industry, health care, education, and other fields, using the same basic material presented in *Antagonists in the Church.* The principles and practices are nearly identical in application, whatever the arena.

How to Use
This Study Guide

*F*OR EACH chapter of *Antagonists in the Church* this study guide contains a number of questions designed to help participants internalize, assimilate, extend, and apply the information in the chapter. Before each session, members of the group should read the chapters to be discussed in that session and review the corresponding questions in this guide. Responding in writing to the questions will better prepare participants to contribute thoughtfully to the group discussion. These written responses, supplemented by notes you take in class, could become a valuable source for continuing reference.

We strongly recommend that you proceed through the material sequentially rather than going straight to what seems most pertinent to the situation you find yourself in. Later chapters build on earlier ones.

As you work in your group, keep in mind who else in the congregation ought to study this material. The fact that God calls the church to be a sign and example of the peaceable kingdom to come makes this a beneficial course for *all* church members.

Materials

Each participant will need a copy of the book *Antagonists in the Church* and a copy of this study guide. Bibles should be available, since some questions refer to specific passages of Scripture. The leader will need access to a chalkboard, a flipchart, or an overhead projector for use in recording ideas from the group.

Leadership

The main task of the leader is to guide the group through the questions, ensuring that the discussion stays on track and moves along at a timely pace. A member of the church staff or a lay person with competent leadership skills can serve as leader.

A competent leader will know when to honor silence as thinking time and when to move on to the next question. A competent leader will draw out those who do not readily express their opinions. A competent leader will avoid extending the discussion of a question beyond the point of any useful return.

A team approach to leadership can also be effective because each member of the leadership team will bring a different perspective and style. If team leadership is adopted, all members of the leadership team should make it a point to attend all group sessions.

Participation in this course can also be seen as leadership training for future offerings of it. One or two of the current participants might be the logical persons to lead a subsequent study group.

Participants

Any adult member of a congregation could be a participant in a study of *Antagonists in the Church;* many should be. During the development and piloting of this course, study groups were drawn from church boards, committees, and councils, deacons and elders. Other groups were established as special adult education offerings in congregations. Some churches used the course as continuing education for their Stephen Ministers. Seminary classes and Clinical Pastoral Education groups have also used this course.

All members of a church staff would be appropriate participants in a study group, as would lay leaders from the governing body of the church. Initially, some church leaders may have strong reservations about the advisability of dealing with the subject at all. Such concerns need to be addressed directly. The course can be described as one helpful way of equipping leaders for their roles. The content of the material should resolve any doubts they might still have about the value of the course.

Having a whole leadership group take part in the course is beneficial because experiences and insights emerge from the collective wisdom of the group. Moreover, since mutual support is the most effective counter to antagonism in the church, a group of individuals working through this course together will begin to develop the cohesion and understanding necessary to be a shield and armor as well as a healing force. Having the entire membership of a church board or committee as participants is particularly useful when an antagonist's activities impinge on their area of responsibility.

Congregations would be well-advised to offer this course on an ongoing basis. As lay leaders change, new leaders should be routinely educated and equipped to deal with antagonists as preparation for their important role.

The study groups could be "by-invitation-only," drawing participants from elders, deacons, executive board members, church staff, or various combinations of these. They could also be part of the regular church educational programming, with an invitation extended to the entire congregation. A church will receive the most benefit from having as many members as possible take part.

Duration and Schedule of the Course

The groups that piloted this course took from as few as 4 to as many as 18 hours to complete it, with the average being in the 10-12 hour range. Some groups spread the study over a number of weeks, while others completed it in two or three longer sessions. The question of scheduling breaks down into several subsidiary questions:

• How frequently shall the group meet?

- What overall length of time will the group spend in this course?
- How long shall each session be?

As you consider what is best for your situation, here are some factors to take into account:

1. Participants need time to read the material and answer the questions before discussing the chapters.
2. How urgent is the situation? If you have scheduled this group study because an antagonist is or may be already at work, that will preclude leisurely examination of the material the first time through.
3. You may be considering studying the book as part of the regularly scheduled meetings of a board or committee. If so, keep in mind that infrequent, poorly attended or irregularly scheduled meetings will all conspire to limit the effectiveness of the study.

One good plan is to schedule six sessions, one a week, and aim to work through four chapters at each session. This is a manageable reading load for most people. You need not be a slave to the "four chapters in each session" agenda. Chapters such as 8 on the "Red Flags of Antagonism" or 16 on "How to Conduct One-to-One Interviews with Antagonists" might require more detailed study than others.

Sessions lasting two and a half hours, including a midpoint break, have worked well. (An important but neglected aspect of leadership in some church settings is to make sure that meetings start and end on time.)

Another possibility is to schedule one or more retreats. If you plan retreats, be sure participants have enough time prior to the event to read through the book and ponder the questions in the study guide. Two one-day retreats, devoted to Parts One and Two and Parts Three and Four respectively, would make the preparatory reading more manageable. A combination of evening sessions with an intervening or concluding retreat is also a workable arrangement.

Attendance

All participants need to attend every session for effective learning. Some congregations have made attendance at their educational programming mandatory and have been pleasantly surprised by how people welcome evidence that Christian education is a significant undertaking.

Group Process

Effectively dealing with antagonists is a difficult and sometimes painful process. Denial, fear, and discomfort all work to an antagonist's advantage, but to the disadvantage of the church. Any Christian striving to live out the love of Christ must wrestle with how to reconcile that love with the need to be firm, sometimes confrontive.

The book *Antagonists in the Church* does not shy away from this need for firmness. As a result, some participants may feel uncomfortable. Here the group process will be of great benefit. Participants will have ample time to discuss, work together, share their experiences, and jointly apply their new understandings.

Generally speaking, this study guide includes more questions for each chapter than you will have time for. Pick and choose among them, looking for ones you feel will be most productive for the group. Not all questions have immediately apparent "answers." Some are simply intended to stimulate thinking. Participants will find answers to the questions both in the text and within the collective experience and wisdom of the group.

The group and its leader(s) need to be particularly sensitive to two aspects of group process: *argumentativeness* and *disagreement by silence.*

• *Argumentativeness.* In group discussions, some participants try the patience of the group by their defense of or attack on particular ideas. *Argument* is a fine and hallowed means of testing the truth of certain propositions; *argumentativeness* is more often determination to be right.

After a period of discussion, it might be well for group members *to agree to disagree* and move on. In all likelihood the issue will be clarified by later chapters.

One of the best strategies for dealing with argumentativeness is for the leader to keep the pace of the group moving. In general, it is better for group members to be hungering for more time to discuss a question than it is for them to be covertly looking at their watches, shuffling papers, and wishing the leader would get on to a new question or another chapter.

• *Disagreement by silence.* Group members and the leader(s) bear mutual responsibility for keeping especially attuned to those in the group who are contributing little or nothing to the discussion. Some people don't want to rock the boat, perhaps because they feel sheepish about disturbing the apparent unanimity of the group. By their silence they may be announcing, "I don't buy into this [whatever the subject of the discussion is] at all." The group needs to draw those people out, for it is by discussion of such firmly held convictions that understanding will be refined and clarified for all.

Skill Practice

A few of the questions in this guide call for role playing by participants in order to practice skills. Group members can increase the success of these exercises by establishing an atmosphere of openness and trust within the group. Here are some points to keep in mind:

1. Encourage volunteers to take the parts. Some people are not comfortable with being "on stage."
2. The leader can state to all that this is a learning opportunity. Perfection is not expected. Critiques after the role plays should be offered as insights into how to deal with antagonists, not as "mistakes" made by those playing the roles.
3. Give people playing the parts a few moments to contemplate their roles before they are asked to begin.

Going Forth

YOU DO NOT enter into this study unassisted or alone, even if you are undertaking it on an individual basis. The good news, the tremendous news, is in Jesus' words to his disciples (and to you):

These things I have spoken to you, while I am still with you. But the Counselor, the Holy Spirit, whom the Father will send in my name, he will teach you all things, and bring to your remembrance all that I have said to you (John 14:25-26).

These words of our Lord should not be interpreted as an excuse for us to simply bide our time and wait for inspiration. They are rather his assurance that the illumination we need will come.

You must still apply your reasoning ability to gain a full understanding of the nature of antagonism. Give as full an answer to each question as you can. Be prepared to bring to the group other questions that occur to you as you read *Antagonists in the Church.*

You are by no means alone.

Chapter 1:
Hope Is the Beginning

1. What do you want to learn from this book? List three questions you hope will be answered.

   a. _____

   b. _____

   c. _____

   *(**Leader:** You may want to ask participants to share some of their questions. Record these and keep them available throughout the study, referring back to them from time to time.)*

2. Reread the definition of an antagonist on pp. 21-22. In light of this definition, have you ever:
   - witnessed an antagonist in action? What happened? How did you feel about it then? How do you feel about it now?

   - yourself been the victim of an antagonistic attack? What happened? How did you feel then? How do you feel now?

3. On p. 23 the author says the entire congregation is responsible for dealing with antagonists. Do you agree? Why or why not?

4. On p. 24 the author says that a major reason antagonism exists in congregations is apathy. Do you agree? Why or why not?

5. What feelings did you experience as you read the accounts in this chapter of those attacked by antagonists? Why?

6. What about your personal responsibility—where does that begin?

Chapter 2:
What Is Church Antagonism?

1. Did anything in the author's elaboration of the definition of a "church antagonist" sound familiar to you? If so, what?

2. How can the definition of antagonists be helpful in determining who antagonists are *not?*

3. What is the difference between conflict that "builds up" and conflict that "tears down" a congregation?

4. How are the three types of antagonists named in this chapter different from each other? How are they similar? (You might make a chart to see similarities and differences at a glance.)

5. Have you ever witnessed an attack on another person by a "hard-core antagonist"? What happened? How did you feel?

6. Have you ever been the object of an attack by a hard-core antagonist? What happened? How did you feel?

7. How would you distinguish between an activist and an antagonist? Can you name some examples of each from news reports you have heard?

Chapter 3:
Levels of Church Conflict

1. What are some examples of healthy conflict within your congregation?

2. On p. 31 the author says that "On a values scale, conflict is neutral. It can be good or bad, healthy or unhealthy, creative or destructive." How do you feel about conflict? How do you handle it?

3. The following scale suggests various levels of asser-tiveness individuals may have in confronting others. Where would you place yourself on the scale?

Seek out house cats and offer myself as an hors d'oeuvre.	Will fight for my life, but still a mouse.	Able to master house cats.	Tigers respect me, but claw me.	Bring me more tigers!

4. What did the diagrams of the five levels of conflict tell you, if anything?

5. Have you ever related on one level in a conflict situation to someone who was operating on a different level? What happened?

6. How does the quote from M. Scott Peck on p. 36 strike you? Although reading these words could be a source of discouragement, might they also be a source of hope? How?

Chapter 4:
Why Antagonism Happens in Congregations

1. How could knowing that antagonists frequently exhibit displacement help someone deal with an antagonistic attack?

2. What are some ways to help other members of your congregation avoid following an antagonist?

3. On p. 39 the author says that antagonists "find power voids, which they subsequently rush to fill." With the problem that sometimes exists for congregations in filling leadership positions, what could you do if an antagonist is the only one who wants a particular position?

4. The author states on p. 40 that one reason antagonists exist in congregations is that it is within the Christian church that particularly sensitive issues are "openly prayed about, preached about, studied, and discussed." What are your thoughts about this?

5. What are some characteristics of congregations that make them vulnerable to antagonistic attack?

6. How could you help to change the way your congregation operates to make it more difficult for antagonists to gain a foothold?

Chapter 5:
A Biblical Perspective

1. What Bible passages in this chapter took on a new or different meaning for you?

2. Can you think of someone who was both "innocent as a dove but wise as a serpent" in dealing with an antagonist? What are your thoughts and feelings about how that person acted?

3. Summarize a biblical approach to dealing with antagonists.

4. When differences arise, how do you determine when to "turn the other cheek" and when not to? Does John 18:22-23 give you any insight?

5. What is your reaction to the possibility of having to use Matthew 18:15-17 with an antagonist?

6. If the occasion were to arise for a congregation to use the disciplinary measures of Matthew 18:15-17, what attitudes and understandings do you think would be essential?

7. Suppose an antagonist seems repentant, and you offer forgiveness. Then a week later you learn that the person is engaged in the same kind of destructive behavior. What would you do then?

Chapter 6:
A Question of Values

1. Are there examples in your experience that help you distinguish between judgmentalism and discerning judgment? If so, share one.

2. Would you feel guilty confronting an antagonist if it would cause him or her pain? If so, how could you deal with that guilt?

3. What are some short-term implications when a congregation and its leaders deal with an antagonist?

4. What are some long-term implications when a congregation and its leaders deal with an antagonist?

5. Why might doing nothing about an antagonist's attack be the worst and most painful decision?

6. How might the pain of dealing with an antagonist actually lead to growth?

7. What is crucial for you in deciding whether or not to deal with an antagonist?

Chapter 7:
Personality Characteristics of Antagonists

1. Note the author's seven questions on pp. 59-60. Have you experienced or witnessed an antagonistic attack? Share something about that experience (maintaining essential confidentiality) and discuss how each of those questions did or did not apply.

2. The author says antagonists exhibit five general personality characteristics "in extreme form." What are examples of more extreme forms of:

   • *negative self-concept?*

   • *narcissism?*

   • *aggression?*

   • *rigidity?*

   • *authoritarianism?*

3. The author mentions as a pitfall, on p. 60, a possible temptation "to carelessly prejudge others, dehumanizing them as mere categories for identification." How can this danger be minimized?

4. Often people see some of the characteristics of antagonists in themselves. Did you? If so, how are you different from an antagonist?

5. What value—if any—was there for you in reading this chapter? How is it helpful to you to understand the antagonistic personality?

6. Review the personality characteristics described in this chapter. Then choose two individuals from the group to role play—in pantomime—an encounter between an antagonist and a nonantagonist. (Don't use any words—just gestures!)

Chapter 8:
Red Flags of Antagonism

1. On p. 69, the author mentions a side effect of reading this chapter, that for a while you might become overly suspicious. How are you feeling right now in this regard? How do you think your excessive suspicion (if you have any) will turn to *healthy paranoia?*

2. Before you knew of the Nameless Others flag, what would your response have been when someone talked about "the others"? Might that response have played into the hands of an antagonist?

3. How do you distinguish between one who is waving the Predecessor-Downer flag and one who has honest misgivings about a predecessor in a particular position?

4. Suppose you are a member of a committee that is responsible for processing membership transfer requests. Your committee receives a letter of transfer to your congregation containing a communication describing significant antagonistic activities on the part of this person in the other congregation. What might be done?

5. Suppose further that your committee accepts this individual as a member. Soon after this person arrives, he or she invites you to dinner at his or her home. How should you relate to this person?

6. Suppose a member of your congregation hands a church staff person or board chairperson a sizable check and then says, "I hope we won't have any more children's sermons." How should that member be responded to?

Chapter 9:
Warning Signs and
How to Recognize Them

1. Have you ever observed examples of the warning signs discussed in this chapter? If so, which ones?

2. What do you think a person's typical response is to early warning signs? What has been your past response to early warning signs?

3. Have you ever been the object of distorted information? How did it make you feel?

4. Suppose an antagonist accuses you of behaving unbiblically, and that person uses faulty biblical interpretation to back up that accusation. How might you respond?

5. On p. 85, the author says, "One of the most counter-productive courses of action would be to respond with a lengthy, single-spaced letter, refuting the antagonist's accusations point by point." Why would this be ineffectual?

6. In this chapter, the author suggests taking special note when someone alerts you to an individual's past antagonistic activities. Shouldn't even those with past antagonistic track records be considered "innocent until proven guilty"? Why or why not?

7. The author talks about one's "sixth sense" as a valid recognition device. What do you think? Have you ever had sixth-sense feelings regarding one or more antagonistic individuals? Were they justified or not?

8. How can you cross-check what your "sixth sense" tells you?

Chapter 10:
How to Maintain an
Anti-antagonist Environment

1. What do you think Mr. Goodman should have done, and when?

2. Do you think that it is too late for the situation at First Church, Anytown, to be corrected? What would need to happen? What would need to change?

3. What "anti-antagonist environment" methodologies does your congregation already have in place?

4. What else might your congregation do to build an anti-antagonist environment? Are any of the means listed in this chapter applicable to your congregation? What would need to happen for one or more of these to be instituted?

5. What kinds of anti-antagonist methodologies do other congregations use?

6. What are your feelings about developing and using anti-antagonist methodologies?

7. How might the implementation of anti-antagonist methodologies—aside from its benefits for preventing antagonism—have implications for improving a congregation's overall operations and ministry?

Chapter 11:
Educating the Leaders
of the Congregation

1. Suppose an antagonist asks to be placed on a particular church committee or to be placed in nomination for a particular office. What would you do?

2. Suppose you are in a position of leadership in your congregation and a member of the congregation is holding a series of unofficial meetings critically discussing the leadership of the congregation. What would you do?

3. Are there any other individuals or groups in the congregation that might benefit from this study of antagonism? Which ones?

4. What could happen if you start specific education too early?

5. At what point would Mr. Goodman or Rev. Kindly (Chapter 10) have been well-advised to start specific education?

6. How can you prevent specific education from becoming a "witch-hunt"?

7. On p. 99 the author states that, "Christians find it extremely difficult to comment realistically about behavior that deserves such comment." Do you agree? Why or why not?

Chapter 12:
How to Use Authority

1. Where are you when it comes to the ability to take an unpopular stand? Put a mark on the continuum below.

Complete
Mush

Rock
of
Gibraltar

How does your group see you?

2. Why are some people able to take an unpopular stand while others seem to have great difficulty?

3. On p. 102 the author says that "People may not like strong leaders, but they hate weak ones." Do you agree or disagree? Explain.

4. What is your "authority of person"? How have you used your "authority of person" in the past? What happened?

5. What is your "authority of office"? How have you used your authority of office before? What happened?

6. On p. 105 the author says, "Failure to use the authority of your office represents more than just a private decision." Do you agree or disagree? Explain.

7. Suppose that after you and other appropriate persons have successfully handled an antagonistic situation, several people tell you that they think you were very unchristian in your dealings with the individual. What would you say to them?

Chapter 13:
How to Relate to
Dormant Antagonists

1. Do you know of examples where individuals did not behave cautiously toward possible antagonists? What were the results?

2. How can being cautious with dormant antagonists actually be the most caring thing to do overall?

3. The author says on p. 111 that, "Weakness invites and prolongs attack; strength repels it." How can you be strong and not come across as heartless?

4. Suppose an antagonist demands that a special committee be set up to deal with his or her grievances. What do you think should be done?

5. Suppose that a person continually makes trivial complaints about you and your leadership during meetings, and immediately after the meetings wants to be very friendly with you. How do you relate to this person after the meetings?

6. Of all the suggestions in this chapter, which would you be most comfortable with? Which would be most effective?

Chapter 14:
The Value
of a Confessor-Confidant

1. Suppose a pastor you know comes to you and says that he or she is going to quit the ministry because of an antagonist. What would you say or do?

2. Have you ever been a confessor-confidant to another? In what ways did you help? What did you learn from the experience?

3. In what ways might a relatively close friendship be a detriment to a confessor-confidant relationship? How might it be an asset?

4. The author advises pastors to seek confessor-confidant relationships outside the congregation. Why?

5. What are some indications that someone is in need of a confessor-confidant when under the attack of an antagonist?

6. How might your family be of help to the family of another church member who is undergoing an antagonistic attack?

7. What are the implications for you that Jesus is with you in a confessor-confidant relationship?

Chapter 15:
Invisible Antagonists

1. How do you feel about ignoring an antagonist?

2. How do you know when to stop ignoring an antagonist and take definitive steps to do something about the situation?

3. What would others in the congregation be likely to think if you dealt singlehandedly with an antagonist at this point?

4. How could you inform other leaders of the congregation about the activities of an antagonist without: *(a)* attracting too much attention; or *(b)* appearing paranoid yourself?

5. How will you know when a significant number of people share your assessment of an antagonist?

6. Suppose that you have been getting many obscene phone calls in the middle of the night and the caller has refused to identify himself. You are almost positive that the caller is an antagonistic member of your congregation. What should you do?

7. What Bible passages could you turn to when, because of an antagonist's rumblings, your own confidence might need a boost?

Chapter 16:
How to Conduct One-to-One
Interviews with Antagonists

1. Have you ever had a meeting with an antagonist like the one described on p. 126? How did you feel before, during, and after?

2. How do the author's suggestions in this chapter relate to the M. Scott Peck quote on p. 36?

3. Of the many suggestions in this chapter, which would be most difficult for you? Why?

4. During an interview with an antagonist, why would it probably be a waste of time to argue church policy or theology or Scripture interpretations?

5. Role-play a telephone conversation with an antagonist: the antagonist wants to have a meeting with you right now. Discuss the role-play afterward. What went well? What was most difficult?

6. Role-play the sequence of events involved in arrival for a meeting with an antagonist. Discuss the role-play afterward. Were there any especially tricky moments? What might have been handled differently?

7. Role-play the interview itself between an antagonist and a church leader, following the author's suggestions. Discuss the role-play afterward. How did the "antagonist" feel as the interview progressed? How about the church leader?

Chapter 17:
Confidentiality
and Documentation

1. What are the differences between confidential material and information that is appropriate to share with leaders of a congregation?

2. What are the appropriate boards and committees for sharing information about an antagonist's attacks?

3. Suppose that the pastor of a congregation has had several private meetings with an individual who manifests a number of antagonistic red flags. During these meetings, this individual has continued to attack the pastor and his or her ministry. The president of the congregation asks the pastor what has been going on in these meetings. What should the pastor say?

4. Suppose you get a request for a transfer to another congregation from an antagonist in your church. Over a period of time, this individual has done severe damage to the congregation. You are in a position that deals with transfers out. What should you communicate about this person to the other congregation and its pastor?

5. Is documentation of an antagonist's disruptive behavior a caring act? If so, in what way? If not, why not?

6. What are the dangers of documentation? What are the dangers of not documenting antagonists—at least minimally?

Chapter 18:
Public Communications
Regarding Antagonism

1. What are your thoughts about the author's objections to using public communication channels against an antagonist?

2. In your view, which of the objections is most revealing? Why?

3. Have you or someone you observed ever tried to deal with an antagonist through the public communication channels mentioned in this chapter? What happened? How effective was it?

4. What are the channels of public communication in your congregation? Which ones might the leaders of your congregation be most susceptible to misuse in an attempt to combat a possible antagonist?

5. What kind of atmosphere would you create in your congregation if you used public communication channels to combat antagonism?

6. Suppose an antagonist asks to use the congregation's mailing list, supplies, and machines to publish complaints that he or she has about the leadership of the congregation and its ministry. Would you allow this? How would you handle it?

Chapter 19:
Leadership Issues

1. What are the similarities and differences between handling an antagonist one-on-one and in a group?

2. What are some ways to guard against an antagonist receiving positive reinforcement for antagonistic behavior from one or more members of the phalanx?

3. What would you say to a church leader who is unwilling to use sanctioned disciplinary measures to stop an antagonist because he or she believed that others might misinterpret the discipline and leave the church?

4. What are the disciplinary measures available in your church?

5. How might "positive thinking" about an antagonist's healthy potential actually be a cop-out?

6. Have you ever been caught in the "perfectionism trap"? Explain.

7. Why do you think church leaders seem particularly vulnerable to the perfectionism trap?

Chapter 20:
Personal
and Family Variables

1. Was there ever a time when you could have identified with one of the stories in the opening of this chapter?

2. What are some things that you do to let off steam when pressures make you anxious and irritable?

3. How can cultivating a solid devotional and prayer life protect you from antagonists?

4. What are some things you can do to keep lines of communication in your family open?

5. What type of activities could you do with your family to reinforce family cohesiveness?

6. Suppose you are under an antagonist's attack (at church or at your place of work), which is causing a great deal of anxiety and stress for you. Your family begins telling you that you are neglecting them. What should you do?

Chapter 21:
Denominational
Support Structures

1. What are the implications for a congregation of involving denominational officials too early in dealing with antagonists? For its lay leaders? Its staff? For denominational officials?

2. On page 168 the author states, "Notify early, but request help late." When is *late?* What's the difference between *late* and *too late?*

3. For skill practice, try reporting an event evaluatively. Then try another event, reporting descriptively. If you are in a study group, stage an event and have half the group report evaluatively, half descriptively (see pp. 169-170).

4. What resources does your denomination have for helping congregations to deal with antagonists?

5. How have denominational representatives been involved in turning back the attack of an antagonist in your congregation or in another congregation with which you have been affiliated?

6. What are some biblical examples of emissaries sent by "denominational leaders" to help a congregation overcome certain struggles?

Chapter 22:
To Leave or Not to Leave

1. On a scale of 1 to 10 (10 being high), rate the importance you place on receiving approval.

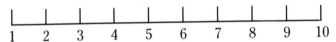

| | | | | | | | | | |
|1|2|3|4|5|6|7|8|9|10|

Other's
approval
does not
concern me.

Need 100%
approval
to operate.

2. Suppose that you and your family have been so hurt by the attacks of an antagonist that you do not think you can remain in your congregation. You want to be honest about the reasons for your decision. How would it be good for you to do this? What reasons would you give for leaving?

3. How might a resignation cause more problems than it solves, both for you and for the board, committee, or congregation you serve?

4. Do you know of anyone whose only alternative to continuing to suffer from the attacks of an antagonist was to resign his or her position of leadership? Why was resignation the only alternative? What could others have done to help? Could the resignation have been prevented through active support of others?

5. The author states that the real issue in considering whether or not to remain in a position is whether effectiveness has been lost. What might be some indications that this has indeed happened?

6. What are some considerations, other than effectiveness, that might need to be addressed before one makes a decision?

Chapter 23:
The Aftermath

1. If you have been involved in an antagonistic attack, how did you feel when it ended? What were the effects on the congregation resulting from the attack?

2. If you found yourself angry toward those who "fell in" with the antagonist, how might you overcome your hostility in order to relate and minister to them?

3. How have other church leaders that you have known cared for themselves after an antagonistic attack?

4. The author suggests a "forgive but don't forget" attitude toward antagonists. Is it really possible to forgive but not forget?

5. What might the leadership of your congregation do to prevent an antagonist from doing the same thing in the future?

6. There is no such thing as a "former" antagonist. Do you agree? Why or why not? What do those who have had experience with antagonists say?

7. Suppose that after your congregation has dealt successfully with an antagonist, he or she comes to you and says that he or she is quitting the congregation. How would you respond to this?

Chapter 24:
The Last Temptations

1. As a result of reading this book, what possible short-range actions are required of you? Of the whole leadership group in your congregation? Make a step-by-step plan.

2. What long-range actions are required of you? Of the whole leadership group? Make a step-by-step plan.

3. Refer to the questions you had hoped you would learn the answers to, written in Chapter 1 of this guide. Have they been answered? Put any unanswered questions to the group for discussion.

4. What is the dominant feeling you now have toward antagonists? What scriptural verses speak to this feeling?

5. Compose a prayer of compassion for antagonists.

6. Close your time together as a group with prayers for
   strength and encouragement for each other.